THE CHANGING CLIMATE OF

NORTH
AMERICA

Patricia K. Kummer

EUROPE

ASIA

NORTH
AMERICA

AFRICA

SOUTH
AMERICA

AUSTRALIA

Cavendish
Square

New York

ANTARCTICA

Published in 2014 by Cavendish Square Publishing, LLC
303 Park Avenue South, Suite 1247, New York, NY 10010

Library of Congress Cataloging-in-Publication Data
Kummer, Patricia K.
The changing climate of North America / by Patricia K. Kummer.
p. cm. — (Climates and continents)
Summary: "Provides comprehensive information on the geography, wildlife, peoples, and climate of the continent of North America and the changes taking place there as a result of climate change"—Provided by publisher.
Includes index.
ISBN 978-1-62712-452-2 (hardcover) ISBN 978-1-62712-453-9 (paperback) ISBN 978-1-62712-454-6 (ebook)
1. Climatic changes — Environmental aspects — North America. I. Kummer, Patricia K. II. Title.
QC982.8 K86 2014
577.2—dc23

Editorial Director: Dean Miller
Senior Editor: Peter Mavrikis
Copy Editor: Cynthia Roby
Art Director: Jeffrey Talbot
Designer: Amy Greenan
Photo Researcher: Alison Morretta
Production Manager: Jennifer Ryder-Talbot
Production Editor: Andrew Coddington

The photographs in this book are used by permission and through the courtesy of: Cover photo by © Steve Skjold/Alamy, Davor Pukljak/Shutterstock.com; Davor Pukljak/Shutterstock.com, 4; Mapping Specialists, 6; David Frazier/Stone/Getty Images, 8; is Cheadle / All Canada Photos / SuperStock, 9; Jad Davenport/National Geographic/Getty Images, 10; Mapping Specialists, 13; age fotostock / SuperStock, 14; Peter Van Rhijn/All Canada Photos/Getty Images, 15; Russell Young/AWL Images/Getty Images, 16; Stephen Saks/Lonely Planet Images/Getty Images, 18; Dave Blackey/All Canada Photos/Getty Images, 19; Purestock/Getty Images, 22; Stefano Paterna / age fotostock / SuperStock, 24; FERNAND BIBAS/AFP Creative/Getty Images, 26; Steven Kazlowski / Science Faction / SuperStock, 28; Oxford Scientific/Oxford Scientific/Getty Images, 29; Visuals Unlimited, Inc./Robert Pickett/Visuals Unlimited/Getty Images, 30; Steven Kaufman/Peter Arnold/Getty Images, 31; © F. Jack Jackson / Alamy, 34; Hinrich Baesemann/picturealliance/dpa/AP Images, 34; Albert Moldvay/Contributor/National Geographic/Getty Images, 36; Ulrike Welsch/Photo Researchers/Getty Images, 37; Perry Mastrovito/First Light/Getty Images, 39; AP Photo/Manuel Balce Ceneta, 40; Michele Falzone/Photographer's Choice/Getty Images, 41.

Printed in the United States of America

CONTENTS

THE NORTHERNMOST CONTINENT

ONE

Looking at a globe or at a world map, it is quite easy to identify the seven **continents**. They are Earth's largest land areas. North America is the third-largest continent. Only Asia and Africa are larger. In order of size, the other four continents are South America, Antarctica, Europe, and Australia.

Getting To Know North America

North America covers about 17 percent of Earth's land area. It reaches farther north than any other continent. The Arctic Ocean forms North America's northern boundary. The Atlantic Ocean lies to the east. The Gulf of Mexico and Caribbean Sea form part of North America's southern boundary. At the continent's southeastern point, Panama's eastern border separates North America from South America. In the northwest,

(Opposite) This photo taken from a satellite in space shows the location and the vast size of North America. Ice-covered land and water (white) in the north contrasts greatly with forested land (green) farther south.

POLITICAL MAP OF NORTH AMERICA

Where in the World Is North America?

MAPPING SKILLS

Use the political map on page 6 to answer the following questions about the continent of North America:

1. What continent lies northwest of North America?

2. What continent lies northeast of North America?

3. Which regions are closest to South America?

4. Which region has the largest countries? Name the countries.

5. Which region is bordered by the Arctic, Atlantic, and Pacific oceans?

This man belongs to the Taos Pueblo group of Native Americans. Their homes, made of adobe brick, are well suited to the United States' southwestern deserts.

the Bering Strait separates North America from Asia.

North America is made up of twenty-three independent countries. Some islands in the Caribbean and in the Atlantic Ocean belong to the United States or to European countries. For example, Greenland, which is the world's largest island, belongs to Denmark. The US Virgin Islands, located in the Caribbean Ocean, belong to the United States.

North America's landmass is sometimes divided into three regions—Northern America, Central America, and the Caribbean. Each region has unique climate, land, or population features. For example, Central America has a tropical climate. The main language spoken there is Spanish. The Caribbean also has a tropical climate but is completely made up of islands.

Because of North America's location and large size, the continent has many landforms and climate zones. They range from the dry, bitter-cold Arctic to the wet, warm, and tropical Caribbean. In turn, North America's

This girl and her mother and grandmother are First Nation people in western Canada.

climates and landforms provide **habitats** for many plants and animals.

Among the continents, North America's population size ranks fourth after Asia, Africa, and Europe. The people of North America belong to several hundred **ethnic groups**. People in most of those groups can trace their families' histories to Africa, Asia, or Europe. Other North Americans are indigenous (native) people. Their families' histories go back to North America's first inhabitants. Native Americans in the United States and First Nation people in Canada are two large groups of native people. The Lenca of Central America and the Arawak of the Caribbean are smaller groups of native people.

The Continents and Change

For hundreds of millions of years, North America and the other continents have undergone slow, continuous change. In fact about 250 million years ago, there was only one continent—Pangaea. Gradually, Pangaea broke apart, and the seven continents that we know were formed. About 3 million years ago, North America achieved the shape that it has today.

9

Volcanic Island Hopping

Many Caribbean islands were formed by volcanic eruptions under the sea. Today, volcanic mountains rise up on those islands. Some of the volcanoes are extinct, or no longer active. Others continue to erupt.

The volcanoes and their eruptions helped create each island's environment. For example, lava has colored the beaches' sands tan, gray, or black. Today, visitors enjoy the beaches, hike up the volcanic mountains, and explore the volcanoes' craters.

The Quill is an extinct volcano on St. Eustatius. Today, a rainforest grows in its crater. Hikers can take a winding trail into the crater among ferns, wild orchids, and giant elephant ears. They might also see a huge gray-green iguana that is now endangered.

In 1995 on Montserrat, the Soufrière Hills volcano began erupting. It continues to spew ash and lava. The lava flows have extended Montserrat's beaches and warmed the waters.

Dominica's volcanoes provide water features. Near one beach, warm water bubbles from volcanic vents under the Caribbean's floor. At another beach, divers explore the crater of an extinct underwater volcano.

Because Earth's crust is made up of many **tectonic plates**, its surface and continents continue to change. These hard, rigid sheets of rock are always moving. Tectonic movement builds mountains and volcanoes. It also causes earthquakes and volcanic eruptions. Along the San Andreas Fault in California, two plates are pushing against each other. Earthquakes frequently occur along that fault.

Another change that concerns North America and the other continents is **climate change**. The main cause of climate change is the release of large amounts of carbon dioxide (CO_2) into the air. Natural events, such as volcanic eruptions, and human actions add to the amount of CO_2. The rise in CO_2 levels in the air is traced to the Industrial Revolution. In the 1800s, North Americans began burning large amounts of coal to run the machines in their factories. Coal continues to be used today, as well as oil, natural gas, and gasoline. All of those fuels give off CO_2.

North Americans also contributed to climate change by altering their natural environment. Large areas of forests, which absorb CO_2, were cut down. In their place, crops were planted, mines were dug, and cities were built. Those actions increased the amount of CO_2 in the air, bringing warmer temperatures and varying rainfall. Now, North America's leaders and individual people are working to improve the environment. Their actions are bringing still more changes to North America.

TALL MOUNTAINS, GREAT PLAINS, HUGE WATERWAYS

North America is famous for its snowcapped Rockies and fertile Great Plains. Some of its longest rivers are the Mackenzie, Mississippi, Missouri, and Rio Grande. Great Bear Lake, the Great Lakes, and Lake Nicaragua are a few of its largest lakes. Bays, gulfs, seas, peninsulas, and islands create North America's long coastline.

Major Mountain Ranges

North America has two main areas of mountain ranges. The Appalachian Mountains are in eastern North America. They extend from Newfoundland in Canada into Alabama in the United States. The Appalachians are North America's oldest and lowest mountains. Erosion from wind and water continue to wear them down. Large coal deposits lie in the Appalachians.

ASIA

ARCTIC OCEAN

EUROPE

Bering Sea

Bering Strait

Yukon River Delta

Yukon River

Mackenzie River Delta

Baffin Bay

Alaska Range

Mt. McKinley (Denali) 20,320 ft (6,194m)

Gulf of Alaska

Mackenzie River

Great Bear Lake

Great Slave Lake

Hudson Bay

Elevations in North America

Feet		Meters
Over 10,000		Over 3,050
5,001–10,000		1,526–3,050
2,001–5,000		611–1,525
1,001–2,000		306–610
0–1,000		0–305
Below sea level		Below sea level

▲ Mountain peak

＼ Dam

+ Depression

Country boundary

State/Province boundary

0   500   1,000 miles

0   500   1,000 kilometers

Lambert Azimuthal Equidistant Projection

COAST MOUNTAINS

ROCKY MOUNTAINS

GREAT

CANADIAN SHIELD

Columbia River

Columbia Plateau

Continental Divide

Lake Winnipeg

Lake Itasca

Lake Superior

Lake Huron

St. Lawrence River

CASCADE RANGE

COAST RANGES

Sierra Nevada

Great Basin

Great Salt Lake

Missouri River

Lake Michigan

Lake Ontario

APPALACHIAN MTS.

Mojave Desert

Colorado Plateau

Lake Powell

P L A I N S

Lake Erie

White Mountains

Grand Canyon

Ohio River

Death Valley -282 ft (-86m)

Lake Mead

Arkansas River

Sonoran Desert

Colorado River

PACIFIC OCEAN

Chihuahuan Desert

Rio Grande

Mississippi River

C O A S T A L   P L A I N

ATLANTIC OCEAN

Sierra Madre Occidental

Sierra Madre Oriental

Mexican Plateau

Apalachicola River

Mississippi River Delta

Apalachicola River Delta Everglades

Gulf of Mexico

Grijalva River Delta

Grijalva River

Caribbean Sea

Lake Nicaragua

NORTH AMERICA

SOUTH AMERICA

N W E S

PHYSICAL MAP OF NORTH AMERICA

The Great Smoky Mountains are located in the southeastern United States. They are part of the Appalachian Mountain system, which was formed about 500 million years ago.

North America's western mountain ranges stretch from northern Alaska through Central America. Those ranges have North America's tallest and youngest mountains. Mount Denali (Mount McKinley) is North America's highest point. It rises 20,320 feet (6,194 m) above sea level in the Alaska Range. Two other large mountain ranges are the Rockies and the Sierra Madre. Large deposits of gold, silver, copper, coal, and aluminum lie in those mountains. Forests grow on their slopes. West of the mountains, a few of North America's largest cities, such as Seattle, Washington and Los Angeles, California, hug the coast.

As far south as Mexico, **glaciers** cover many of the western mountains. Volcanoes formed some of the western mountains and most mountains on islands in the Caribbean. From Alaska to Panama and on Caribbean islands, active volcanoes continue to rumble and occasionally erupt.

Plateaus and Deserts

Several plateaus, or high and somewhat flat land, stand between the western mountain ranges. The largest plateaus include the Columbia, Colorado, and Mexican. Major rivers cut across them. Crops and grasses grow well on the plateaus. Cattle graze on their grasses. North America's largest city, Mexico City, is on the Mexican Plateau.

Glaciers on the Canadian Shield smoothed these granite slabs that lie in Lake Huron in Ontario, Canada.

North America's deserts are also found between the western mountain ranges. From largest to smallest, the main deserts are the Chihuahuan, Sonoran, and Mojave. Another desert area is the Great Basin. It is called a basin because none of its rivers flow to the ocean. Instead, they all flow into the Great Salt Lake. One part of the Great Basin is quite low. In fact, North America's lowest point is there. Death Valley in California lies 280 feet (86 m) below sea level.

Another large plateau is the Canadian Shield. It reaches from the Arctic Ocean to the Great Lakes. Volcanic rock covers much of the land. Deposits of gold, silver, copper, zinc, and diamonds lie under the rock. Thick forests grow on the southern part of the Canadian Shield.

Coastal and Interior Plains

A narrow strip of coastal plain extends east of the Appalachians to the Atlantic Ocean. Another coastal plain lies along the Gulf of Mexico from Florida through Mexico. North America's wide interior plain pushes against the continent's two mountainous areas and the Canadian Shield. The western part of the interior plain is called the Great Plains. Some of the continent's largest rivers flow through the interior plain. Many of North America's largest cities, such as New York City and Chicago, rise along the coastal plain and above the interior plain.

North America's plains have some of the world's richest soil. The coastal plains produce large crops of vegetables, fruits, peanuts, cotton, sugarcane, and rice. The eastern interior plain yields huge amounts of soybeans and corn. The Great Plains are known for large harvests of barley, hay, oats, sugar beets, and wheat. Cattle and sheep graze on Great Plains grassland. Large deposits of coal, iron ore, natural gas, and petroleum lie under the Great Plains.

Rivers, Lakes, and Coastlines

The Continental Divide runs along the eastern edge of North America's western mountains. It extends from Canada through Central America. Rivers west of the Great Divide flow into the Pacific Ocean. Rivers east of the Great Divide flow into the Arctic Ocean, the Atlantic Ocean, or the Gulf of Mexico. Many of North America's longest rivers, including the Mississippi, flow into the Gulf of Mexico.

Huge hay fields span this part of the Great Plains in Montana—the fourth largest of the states.

Before North America's rivers empty into a sea or ocean, some form a delta (a wide triangle of land). The buildup of soil on the Apalachicola Delta supports sea grasses. Forests cover the Yukon Delta. The Mississippi, Mackenzie, and Grijalva deltas are sources of natural gas and petroleum deposits.

North America's rivers often flood because of heavy rain or melting snow. Floodwaters deposit rich soil in the river valleys. But floods can also damage crops, farmland, homes, and city streets. To prevent floods, North Americans have built more than 80,000 dams on the continent's rivers. Many dams also produce hydroelectric power for North America's cities, towns, and farms.

North America is dotted with thousands of freshwater lakes. The state of Minnesota alone has more than 10,000. Lake Superior is the world's largest freshwater lake. It is one of the five Great Lakes that lie between Canada and the United States. The other Great Lakes are Huron, Michigan, Erie, and Ontario. The Great Lakes contain 20 percent of the

A Trip down the Mississippi River

The Mississippi is North America's longest river. It begins at Lake Itasca in northern Minnesota. The mighty Mississippi starts as a narrow stream. It is only about 20 to 30 feet (6–9 m) wide and barely 2 feet (0.6 m) deep. Small children easily walk across this part of the river. As the clear Mississippi flows south, it separates Minneapolis from St. Paul in Minnesota. In St. Louis,

Missouri, it picks up the muddy water from the Missouri River. Farther south in Cairo, Illinois, the waters from the Ohio River join the Mississippi. South of Memphis, Tennessee, the Arkansas River flows into the Mississippi. Finally, not far from New Orleans, Louisiana, the Mississippi empties into the Gulf of Mexico. At that point, the river is several miles wide and about 45 feet (14 m) deep. The full length of the Mississippi is 2,340 miles (3,765 km).

Up and down the river, barges carry loads of grain, coal, steel, and lumber. Modern-day riverboats carry passengers. Along the way, they see forests, meadows, cotton fields, and towns. They often spot ducks, geese, herons, and pelicans, too.

world's freshwater. In the 1960s, Lake Erie was a dead lake. Pollution from factories and farms had killed most of the lake's plant and animal life. In the 1970s, the governments of Canada and the United States started programs to stop the pollution. By the 1990s, people could again swim and fish in Lake Erie. Many birds

The Mica Dam spans the Columbia River in British Columbia. Its hydroelectric plant delivers power to that Canadian province.

and other animals that migrated because of the pollution also returned to the lake.

Of all the continents, North America has the world's longest coastline at 190,000 miles (305,775 km). Deep bays, gulfs, and harbors cut into its coastal lands. Today, the action of wind and water is eroding all of North America's coasts. Dams on North America's rivers have also caused coastal erosion. Along with water, the dams hold back sand and soil. Dams on the Mississippi are causing the delta to sink. Deltas need the sand and soil to maintain their size and shape.

Getting the Lay of the Land

Study the physical map of North America on page 13 to answer the following questions:

1. What piece of land has the highest elevations?

2. In which direction (north, east, west, or south) does the land become higher in North America?

3. What is the source (beginning) of the Mackenzie River?

4. Locate and name two rivers, other than the Mackenzie, that flow north.

5. What river connects the Great Lakes to the Atlantic Ocean?

ANSWERS:
1. Greenland, or the large island north of Baffin Bay
2. West
3. Great Slave Lake
4. Grijalva, Yukon
5. St. Lawrence

WARMING TEMPERATURES, VARYING RAINFALL

North America is the only continent that has all of the world's climate zones. They range from the dry, bitter-cold Arctic to the warm, wet tropical Caribbean. North America's most extreme temperatures have been 134° F (56° C) in Death Valley, California, and -81.4°F (-62°C) in Snag, Yukon Territory, Canada. North America's annual precipitation (rain and snow) extremes are 276 inches (701 cm) in Henderson Lake, British Columbia, Canada, and 1.2 inches (3 cm) in Batagues, Mexico.

Climate Change in North America

Major differences in temperatures and precipitation over several years are known as climate change. North America's people have been responsible for most of the continent's climate change. Since the 1600s, North Americans made major changes to the land. They cut down forests

The air over Los Angeles is often polluted.

and plowed up grasslands to plant crops. Trees and grasses absorb CO_2. With fewer forests and grasslands, the amount of CO_2 in the air increased. That in turn caused temperatures to increase and rainfall to decrease.

North Americans also built some of the world's largest cities. In some parts of North America, megalopolises (long, continuous stretches of cities and suburbs) developed. Megalopolises are found along parts of the Atlantic and Pacific coasts and along the Great Lakes. These heavily urban areas create heat islands because buildings, streets, and roads now cover the land. North America's cities can be as much as 9°F (5°C) warmer than nearby rural areas.

In addition, homes, apartments, factories, and office buildings in North America's urban areas must be cooled and heated. Air conditioning requires special coolants. Large amounts of coal, oil, and natural gas are burned for heat and for cooking. Many families drive two or more gasoline-powered cars. Buses, trains, and trucks also use gasoline or diesel fuel. All those gases give off CO_2, which adds to climate change.

Results of Climate Change

During the past 100 years, North America has experienced climate change. Overall, temperatures have become warmer by 1.6°F (0.9°C). That is slightly more than the world's average increase of 1.3°F (0.74°C). However, temperatures in northern parts of Alaska and Canada have increased by about 3.6°F (2.1°C).

North America's precipitation has changed, too. Heavier rains have fallen in many parts of eastern Northern America. Less rain has fallen in western parts of Northern America. This has led to **drought** and wildfires in those already dry western areas.

Throughout North America, the warming climate has affected the environment. Glaciers in the Rocky Mountains and atop

How Scientists Measure Climate Change

Throughout North America, scientists use many methods to measure climate change. At weather stations, they read regular thermometers and rain gauges, and record changes in daily and annual weather. They also study growth rings from old trees such as bristlecone pines, which are found in dry regions of the western United States. The rings tell when rainy and dry periods occurred during the past five thousand years. In North America's Arctic, scientists study ice cores. Air bubbles with CO_2 have been trapped in the ice. The gas in the bubbles tells how temperatures have changed through thousands of years.

Costa Rica's Cloud Forest

Costa Rica's mountains contain a rare environment—a cloud forest. Only 1 percent of the world's forestlands are cloud forests. They exist at elevations where moisture-filled clouds hang above the treetops. Costa Rica's cloud forest sits atop mountains on the Continental Divide. Besides the trees, more than 2,500 other kinds of plants soak up the water that drips from the clouds. The cloud forest is thick with mosses, ferns, and more than 400 kinds of orchids.

More than 100 species of mammals live in the cloud forest. They include spider monkeys and six species of cats—jaguars, jaguarundis, margays, ocelots, oncillas, and pumas. About 400 species of birds also make the forest home. They include the colorful quetzal and the strange-sounding, three-wattled bellbird, which is now endangered.

The cloud forest itself is endangered by climate change. As temperatures become warmer, the clouds will move to higher elevations in other areas.

ranges in Alaska are melting at faster rates. In the Arctic Ocean, both the amount of ice and depth of the ice have decreased. Warmer ocean waters have led to a rise of sea level. That in turn has caused flooding and erosion along North America's long coastline.

Natural Disasters

North America frequently experiences natural disasters that are weather related. Many disasters occurred during one week in the summer of 2012. Wildfires blazed west from the Great Plains to parts of the Rocky Mountains. Flooding caused by heavy rainstorms swamped Florida's panhandle area. Thunderstorms with rain and hurricane-force winds tore along the eastern plains. The storms were followed by a heat wave from the Great Plains to the Atlantic Coast. All of those disasters brought death to people, farm animals, and wildlife. They also caused billions of dollars in property damage.

North America is often hit with windstorms. Winter blizzards pack a triple punch—powerful winds, heavy snowfall, and freezing temperatures. They hit the Great Plains and the land along the Great Lakes. Throughout the spring and summer, dark tornado funnels twist across the Great Plains and up the Mississippi River valley. When a tornado touches land, it has the strength to wipe out entire towns. In summer and early fall, hurricanes develop over warm waters in the North Atlantic. In that area, warm, wet air rises and starts spinning. Hurricanes hit land along the Atlantic Coast and the Gulf of Mexico and in the

Hurricane winds can reach speeds of 200 miles (322 km) per hour, resulting in much damage.

Caribbean. Heavy rains from the storms cause severe floods. With ocean waters becoming warmer, hurricanes are occurring more frequently and with fiercer winds.

Tectonic plate movement causes some of North America's natural disasters. Earthquakes and volcanic eruptions occur mainly along the Pacific Coast. Lands there are part of the Ring of Fire—a belt of volcanoes and earthquakes that circles the Pacific Ocean. In recent years, still other areas of North America have felt earthquake tremors. In 2011, a 5.8-strength earthquake rattled the Atlantic Coast. Large buildings in Washington, DC, were damaged. The Caribbean is another area that experiences volcanoes and earthquakes.

North America has forty-four active volcanoes. Sixteen are located in Alaska. The most recent eruptions have occurred in Central America and the Caribbean. Lava from volcanic eruptions destroys nearby property. But lava also enriches the soil. Years later, crops, trees, and other plants again cover the ground.

FOUR

A CHANGING NATURAL ENVIRONMENT

Nature and people have made many changes to North America's land and bodies of water. In turn, those changes have affected the habitats of the continent's plants and animals. Today, about 15 percent of North America's animal species are endangered.

Melting Ice, Thawing Tundra

Climate change has brought warmer temperatures to North America's Arctic Ocean and **tundra**. Every summer more Arctic ice melts. By 2020, some scientists think the Arctic will be completely free of ice in the summer. Polar bears hunt for seals and walruses dive for fish in Arctic waters. With less ice, those animals must swim farther between icy resting spots. Young polar bears often do not survive the long swims.

27

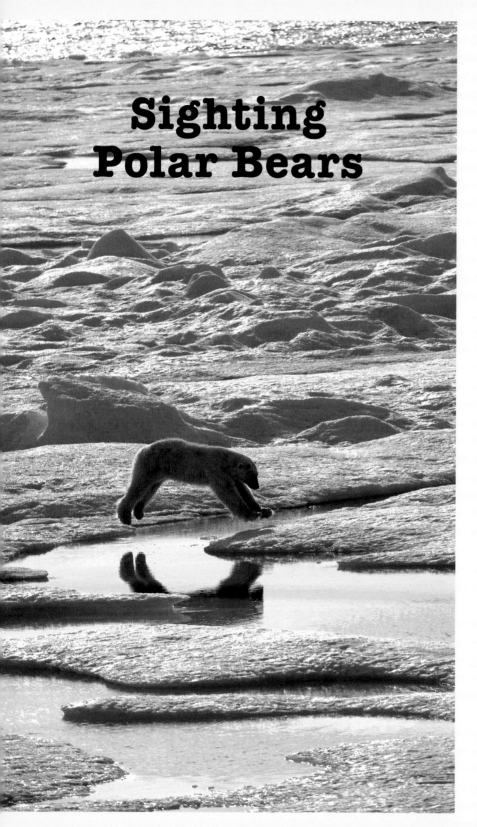

Sighting Polar Bears

Churchill, Manitoba, is on the tundra at the southwestern edge of Hudson Bay. This Canadian town is known as the polar bear capital of the world. It is one of the world's few places to see polar bears in the wild. Each fall, about 1,000 polar bears move into Churchill. Only about 800 people live in the town. When the ice builds up in Hudson Bay, the polar bears hit the water in search of seals.

Land south of North America's Arctic Coast is covered with tundra. Because this land is frozen most of the year, trees cannot grow there. The frozen soil is called **permafrost**. During the summer, the sun shines almost twenty-four hours a day. That allows the top several inches of permafrost to thaw. Then, short shrubs, ferns, grasses, and berries bloom on the tundra. Those plants provide food for caribou, musk oxen, polar bears, and grizzly bears. With increased temperatures, more of the permafrost is thawing. Some tundra plants no longer grow in those conditions. With less food, many animals are becoming endangered.

Restoring Forests

South of the tundra, warmer temperatures and year-round precipitation allow forests to grow. Since the 1600s, **deforestation** has occurred. Farms, mines, and cities replaced the trees. Still, large areas of forest stand throughout the continent. Some of North America's forests have been replanted. Today, laws limit how many trees may be cut.

Mangrove trees once stood along this now-polluted Central American coast.

Northern America's forests have cedar, fir, pine, and spruce trees. Others have leaf-bearing trees such as ash, beech, birch, hickory, oak,

29

These alligators in Everglades National Park are now among Florida's endangered species.

and poplar. Black bears, elk, lynx, moose, mountain lions, and wolves live in these forests. The American bald eagle and Northern spotted owl nest in the trees. The eagle is no longer endangered, but the owl still is.

Tropical rainforests cover much of southern Mexico, Central America, and some Caribbean islands. They receive more than 80 inches (203 cm) of rainfall each year. Tall almond, mahogany, rosewood, spiny cedar, and yellowwood trees are major rainforest trees. Heavy logging has caused many rainforest animals to lose their habitat. The jaguar, North America's largest cat, along with the toucan, Harpy eagle, and many kinds of parrots remain endangered.

Dry and Wet Grasslands

The Great Plains is a huge area of dry grassland. Small shrubs and a few trees grow among the tall and short grasses. Until the 1930s, farmers plowed up the grasses to plant crops. Sometimes the Great Plains experienced long periods of drought. Then the crops died and the land turned to dust. This led to **desertification**. In the western Great Plains, farmers have turned the land back to grasses. A few pronghorn antelope and bison have returned to the Great Plains. Under the plains, prairie dogs build large colonies called "towns" and pop up from their burrows.

The Everglades is marshy, tropical grassland in southern Florida. Large areas of sawgrass prairie cover the Everglades. Alligators build nests in the sawgrass. Bobcats and Florida panthers roam through the area. Farms, cities, and roads continue to push against the Everglades. That development slows the flow of water into the Everglades. Alligators, panthers, and many types of birds are now endangered.

Early settlers in the southwest hunted the ocelot close to the point of extinction. Now, climate change endangers the ocelot population.

Drying Deserts

North America's deserts are found in the southwest. These dry places receive less than 10 inches (25 cm) of rain each year. Joshua trees, mesquite, and many varieties of cacti grow in North America's deserts. Armadillos, bighorn sheep, coyotes, ocelots, northern jaguars, snakes, scorpions, and tortoises also live in the deserts.

Warming temperatures cause even less rain to fall on North America's deserts. Then, fewer plants are able to grow. They no longer provide food or shelter for the deserts' animals. The ocelot, northern jaguar, and tortoise are now endangered.

Lakes, Rivers, and Coastlines

North America's lakes, rivers, and coastlines provide homes for many fish, birds, and other wildlife. Overfishing has decreased the numbers and types of fish, especially Atlantic cod. The governments of some North American countries, such as Canada and the United States, now ban or limit fishing in some areas.

Pollution has also hurt many habitats. Oil leaks from wells, pipelines, and tankers have damaged large areas of the coastline. In 1989, an oil tanker spilled 11 million gallons (42 million l) of oil in the Gulf of Alaska. Sea otters, seals, salmon, and many kinds of birds died. Today, oil remains under the coastline's sand. In 2010, an oil rig exploded in the Gulf of Mexico. About 206 million gallons (780 million l) of oil spilled from the well. More than 4,500 animals died. Some were already **endangered species**, such as the brown pelican and several kinds of sea turtles.

PEOPLE AND CHANGE

North America is a continent of immigrants. About 15,000 years ago, North America's first people walked from Asia. At that time, a land bridge still connected the two continents. Today, many groups of native people can trace their ancestors back to those early immigrants. From the late 1400s to the present day, North America's population groups have expanded. They now include people whose families once lived in Asia, Africa, Europe, and South America.

North America's moderate climate and rich soil have made the continent a good place for people to live. Currently, North America has the world's fourth-largest population. About 542 million people, or 8 percent of the world's people, live in North America. The United States has North America's largest number of people—about 311 million. The Caribbean island country of Saint Kitts and Nevis, with about 50,300 people, has North America's smallest population.

33

An Endangered People – The Arctic's Inuit

The Inuit people live in North America's Arctic. About 100,000 Inuit make their homes in the world's northernmost, coldest area. From Alaska to Canada to Greenland, the Inuit hunt whales, seals, walruses, caribou, polar bears, and grizzly bears. Climate change in the Arctic has decreased the numbers of those animals. Many species have now been declared endangered. That means that the Inuit can no longer hunt those animals.

As the Inuit lose their food supply, they are forced to give up their way of life. Many Inuit have already moved into towns and cities in Alaska and Canada. In the past, most Inuit attended schools in their settlements. They learned to speak and to write English. Many of them continued to speak their native language. Now more Inuit are living in English-speaking communities. Gradually, the Inuit will stop speaking their own language and their children will no longer learn it. The Inuit language will then become extinct.

Changes in Population Growth

North America has one of the world's slower-growing populations. By 2050, the continent's population is expected to increase by only 153 million people. Most of that growth is expected in the United States and Mexico. In the United States, most of the increase will occur from immigration. More than 1 million people come to the United States each year. A high birthrate will help Mexico's population growth. Couples in many Central American and Caribbean countries also have large families.

The main reason for North America's slow population growth is a low birthrate. This is occurring mainly in Canada and the United States. Couples in those countries are having fewer children. Many North Americans graduate from high school and continue on to college. They choose to establish their careers before getting married and having children.

Where North America's People Live

Most of North America's people live in river valleys, along the Great Lakes, and along the Atlantic and Pacific coasts. Those areas have the best farmland. They are also where North America's large cities were built. North America's largest cities are Mexico City, Mexico; New York, Los Angeles, and Chicago in the United States; and Toronto, Canada.

(top) An Inuit family in Greenland wear clothing and boots made of animal skins, covered with traditional designs.
(bottom) An Inuit woman in Canada stays warm in a traditional jacket trimmed with wolf fur.

Mexico City, Mexico — North America's Largest City

Mexico City is Mexico's capital and North America's largest city. More than 9 million people live there. Mexico City is also one of North America's highest cities. It sits 7,350 feet (2,240 m) above sea level on the Mexican Plateau. Mexico City

is one of North America's oldest cities, too. In 1325, the Aztecs built the city of Tenochtitlan on an island in Lake Texcoco. In the 1500s, the Spaniards renamed the city Mexico City.

Since the 1500s, Mexico City's environment has changed. Many years ago, Lake Texcoco was drained. Now the lakebed is completely covered with Mexico City's buildings and roadways. In some places, the city has sunk as much as 30 feet (9 m) into the spongy ground. As the city expanded, trees were cut down. Today, some forests still stand near the city's southern edge.

Most North Americans live in or near cities. That is why North America has one of the world's largest urban populations—about 78 percent. Individual North American countries have even larger percentages of city dwellers. For example, the Bahamas, Canada, and the United States are more than 80 percent urban. North America's urban areas have the continent's best schools and the best-paying jobs. That is why so many people move to its urban areas. By 2030, about 85 percent of North America's people will be living in cities.

Only 25 percent of Cuba's population live on farms or in small villages.

The other 22 percent of North America's population live in rural areas. In some Caribbean countries, that percentage is much higher. For example, about 86 percent of the people in Trinidad and Tobago live in rural areas. In the Caribbean, farming continues to be an important way to make a living. Bananas and other fruits, cacao (chocolate), coffee, cotton, rice, spices, and sugarcane are the main crops. In other parts of North America, fewer people are needed on farms. Those farms use mechanical equipment to plant, weed, and harvest crops.

LOOKING FOR SOLUTIONS TO PRESENT-DAY PROBLEMS

North America still has large areas of livable, usable land. The people of North America are trying to improve the continent's natural environment. They have replanted many forests and restored some grasslands. They are cleaning up polluted waterways and protecting the coastline.

North America's Major Problems

One of North America's problems is the slow-growing population. Overall, the continent has both a low birthrate and a low death rate. That means that North America has fewer young people to support the aging population. In North American, the average life expectancy is about 78 years.

North America, along with the rest of the world, must face the problem of climate change. Throughout the twenty-first century, scientists expect temperatures to rise in every part of the continent. The highest rises are expected in Canada and Alaska in the winter. The southwestern United States and northern Mexico will have the largest increases during the summer. Longer and more frequent heat waves are predicted for all of North America. Heavier rain is predicted for eastern Canada and the

Heavier than usual rainfall flooded this cornfield in eastern Canada.

United States. The Great Plains and southwest will receive less rain and experience more droughts. Most of Northern America will receive less snow, and it will melt earlier in the spring.

Toward a Better Tomorrow

North America does have several things in its favor. The continent's slow-growing population should put less pressure on its land, water, and mineral resources. It might even slow the rate of climate change.

North America also has many well-educated people. Its schools and universities are among the best in the world. They provide leaders for North America's governments and businesses. They also train workers for North America's many industries.

North America is also rich in natural resources. The continent has some of the world's richest soil. It produces large amounts of corn, cotton, oats, potatoes, soybeans, sugar beets, sugarcane, and wheat.

Energy collected from roof-top solar panels helps supply electricity for this home In Northern America.

Florida, California, Central America, and the Caribbean provide most of the world's oranges, grapefruits, lemons, and limes. North America also has many mineral resources. Large amounts of coal and iron ore are mined across Northern America. Northern America is also a major producer of the world's oil and natural gas.

North America also has important sources of natural, clean energy. Geothermal power is a source for electricity. That power comes from heat generated underground by hot springs. Throughout North America, dams on the continent's rivers generate hydroelectric power. Wind farms with wind turbines, or modern-day windmills, are located on land in places with strong, steady winds. Solar panels collect energy from the sun.

Central America and the Caribbean are leaders in wind and solar power. One of those countries has come up with a daring plan. By using clean sources of energy, Costa Rica plans to be carbon neutral by 2021. That country will then absorb as much CO_2 as it emits into the air.

Since 1872, North America's governments have set aside land for national parks and national forests. Hunting, logging, and mining are strictly regulated in those areas. In the 1970s, several governments started passing laws to improve air and water quality. Those laws helped clean up many of North America's rivers and lakes, and made the air clearer in several North American cities.

Grand Canyon National Park

Grand Canyon National Park is located in northern Arizona. More than 1 mile (1.6 km) deep, the Grand Canyon is one of the world's deepest canyons. It is grand in other ways, too. The Grand Canyon is 277 miles (446 km) long and at its widest point spans 18 miles (29 km). About 6 million years ago, the Colorado River started cutting through rock to form the canyon's high walls.

Today, scientists study the different layers of rock in the canyon. They learn about plants and animals that lived in the canyon long ago. Visitors can walk along the canyon's rim or ride a mule to the canyon floor. They might see Bighorn sheep, a coyote, or a California condor. Other visitors float down the Colorado River in rubber rafts.

GLOSSARY

climate change   an increase or decrease in temperature or rainfall over a long period of time

continent   a large land mass

deforestation   cutting down of entire forests

desertification   weakening of soil from deforestation, drought, overuse of land, or climate change

drought   a long period of time with little or no rainfall, making it hard to grow crops

endangered species   a plant or animal that is in danger of becoming extinct

ethnic group	people who share the same national origins, language, and culture
glacier	a large sheet of thick, slowly moving ice and snow
habitat	the natural place in which a plant or animal lives
permafrost	land that is permanently frozen beneath the surface
tectonic plates	the hard sheets of moving rock that make up Earth's crust
tundra	cold, dry, treeless land near the Arctic Ocean

BOOKS   Aloian, Molly. *The Rocky Mountains*. Mountains Around the World. New York: Crabtree Publishing Company, 2011.

Ganeri, Anita. *North America's Most Amazing Animals*. Animal Top Tens. Chicago: Heinemann-Raintree, 2008.

Johnson, Robin. *The Mississippi: North America's River Highway*. Rivers Around the World. New York: Crabtree Publishing Company, 2010.

Royston, Angela and Michael Scott. *North America's Most Amazing Plants*. Plant Top Tens. Chicago: Heinemann-Raintree, 2008.

Woods, Michael. *Seven Natural Wonders of North America*. Seven Wonders. Minneapolis: Twenty-First Century Books, 2009.

Woodward, John. *Climate Change*. Eyewitness Books. New York: DK Publishing, 2008.

DVDS   *Canada's National Parks*. Trailwood Films and Media, 2006.

Globe Trekker: Ultimate Central America. Pilot Productions, 2008.

WEBSITES   **North America: For Kids—National Zoo (FONZ)**
http://nationalzoo.si.edu/audiences/kids
This website has fact sheets, jigsaw puzzles, a migration game, and pages to print and color.

North America Weather
http://weather.org/North America.htm
This page shows current weather conditions across North America, with links to the weather in individual states and regions.

INDEX

ABOUT THE AUTHOR

Patricia K. Kummer has a B.A. in history from St. Catherine University in St. Paul, Minnesota, and an M.A. in history from Marquette University in Milwaukee, Wisconsin. She has written chapters for several world history and American history textbooks and has authored more than sixty books about countries, states, natural wonders, inventions, and other topics. Books she has written for Cavendish Square Publishing include *Working Horses* in the Horses! series and the seven books in the Climates and Continents series.